Greenhaven World History Program

GENERAL EDITORS

Malcolm Yapp
Margaret Killingray
Edmund O'Connor

Cover design by Gary Rees

ISBN 0-89908-208-4 Paper Edition
ISBN 0-89908-233-5 Library Edition

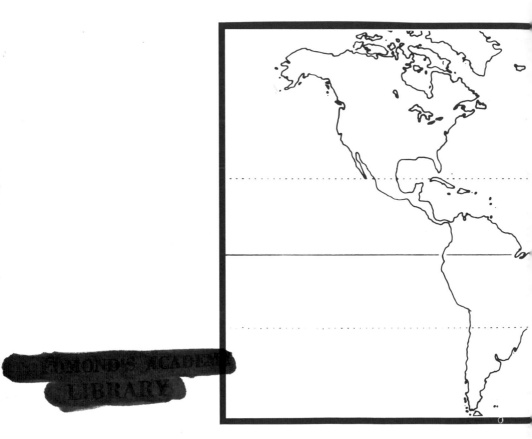

HITLER'S REICH

by Eileen Pearson

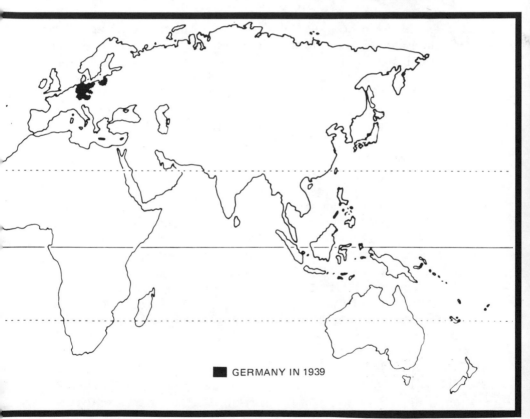

GERMANY IN 1939

Greenhaven Press, Inc.
577 SHOREVIEW PARK ROAD
ST. PAUL, MN 55112

THE THOUSAND YEAR REICH

Germany between 1933 and 1945 was dominated by its Fuhrer (leader), Adolf Hitler. His amazing influence over people needs to be appreciated in order to understand the country and the way it acted during those years. He was appointed Chancellor (Chief Minister) in January, 1933, and eighteen months later Germany was completely in his power. The country prospered and its people grew confident. Hitler boasted that his Reich (state or kingdom) would last for a thousand years — longer even than the Roman Empire. It lasted for only twelve! After winning dramatic victories in the early part of the Second World War, the Germans were totally defeated in 1945. Their land was occupied by foreign troops, and was divided into the two states of East and West Germany. Twelve years is a short time in a country's history but the twelve years of Hitler's Reich were a time of excitement and change, of triumph, suffering and defeat on a grand scale. What happened in Germany then, upset the order of Europe and affected the lives of millions of people across the world.

WHAT SORT OF A MAN WAS HITLER?

As Fuhrer, Hitler became the idol of millions of Germans. His vast rallies drew thousands of spectators. He had a gift for swaying an audience that seemed almost magical. Many people who met him fell under his spell. This is especially surprising as he was so ordinary looking. (D1)* He was a man of extreme moods. His charm could give way to rage. Then he would shout, weep and bang his fists on the table. His energetic activity could give way to suicidal depression.

His official life story told of early struggles against poverty. In fact he had a comfortable home in a small town in Austria where his father was a customs official. Hitler failed his exams through laziness. He was a difficult boy with few friends. He went to Vienna, the capital of Austria, at nineteen. The city was growing rapidly and many of its new arrivals were discontented. Some looked for people to blame for their misfortunes and for no real reason hit upon the many Jews there. Hitler, too, learned to hate the Jews and to believe that violence could settle all problems. Later he went to Germany to escape Austrian army service.

He actually enjoyed the 1914-18 war, and won the Iron Cross for bravery. Feeling betrayed and angry when Germany surrendered, he joined the small National Socialist Party (Nazis) and became a successful and emotional public speaker. He was fascinated by the power of words which became his strongest weapon. (D2) He wrote *Mein Kampf* (My Struggle) in prison after failing to take over the government in Munich in 1923. It contained the idea that the Germans were a master-race destined to rule the world.

His chance came in the days of despair and unemployment following the depression of 1929. *(A World Economy)** His belief in a

*The reference (D) indicates the numbered documents at the end of this book
**Titles in brackets refer to other booklets in the Program

Adolf Hitler in uniform wearing the Iron Cross

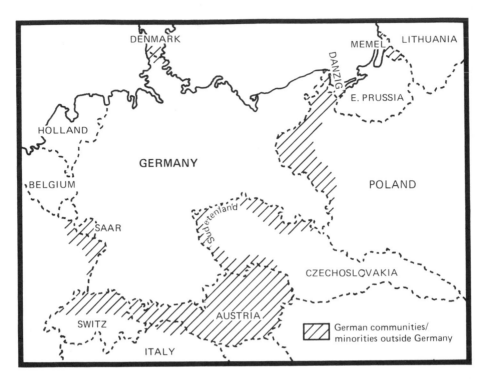

Germany in 1933

Map labels: DENMARK, MEMEL, LITHUANIA, DANZIG, E. PRUSSIA, HOLLAND, GERMANY, POLAND, BELGIUM, SAAR, Sudetenland, CZECHOSLOVAKIA, SWITZ, AUSTRIA, ITALY

German communities/ minorities outside Germany

revived Germany won him much support, especially from those who feared that the communists might take over unless he did. Some of these men helped him to take power. He enjoyed immense success and popularity in the 1930s. He was pictured as a typical German, a country-lover fond of children and dogs. In fact, he was a strange, awkward man whose strongest bond was with the crowds. His effect on them was sometimes startling. (D3) Reichs-marshal Goering remarked that his followers loved Hitler and regarded him as being sent by God to save Germany.

At first he was successful in everything. Defeat in war, when it finally came in Russia in 1942, was unbelievable. He scarcely spoke in public again. He could not conduct a defensive campaign. He refused to hear of retreat, yelled that the Russians were all dead, and ordered the army to advance. German soldiers died in thousands. Disillusioned army officers plotted to kill Hitler but failed. He began to go downhill rapidly, believing the German people had betrayed him. Drugged and half-crazed, he lived in the underground shelters in the Berlin Chancellery. He married Eva Braun, his companion and mistress for many years. They committed suicide as the Russians closed in and their bodies were burned.

4

WHAT WAS GERMANY LIKE IN 1933?

The country was in a desperate state in 1933. Six million people were out of work. Hitler alone spoke of recovery. People blamed the government. The democratic Republican government, set up in 1919 after Germany's defeat in the First World War, had signed the Treaty of Versailles. *(The Two World Wars)* The terms of the Treaty were considered unjust and were said to make it difficult for industry to recover. The Social Democratic Party supported the Republic but the Communists and the Nationalists were unenthusiastic. Before 1933 Hitler's Nazi party won over most supporters of other nationalist parties and became the largest single party. It won the support of most Germans, however, only after it had taken power.

In Germany the government had more control of the economy than in most west European countries. It controlled the banks, power supply and transport. It helped to fix prices and was important in the trade unions and employers' associations. A dictator would find it easy to take over.

The 'unalterable party programme' of the Nazis appealed to many people with its socialist ideas, but it was with the Nationalists that Hitler formed a government in 1933. Businessmen were promised their companies would not be touched. His greatest support came from people weary of poverty and poor leadership, and frightened of the Communists. He promised work and bread, and a new proud future for Germany. His energy and personality gave them confidence.

SECURING POWER

Hitler wanted power. However, he was an elected leader and could be voted out. So he had to destroy democracy. The Reichstag helped him in this. Its building had already gone, badly damaged in a fire of February 1933. Its most outspoken

Judges in a Nazi court

Party Organization

A. OFFICIALS IN CHARGE OF PARTY ACTIVITIES

42 Gauleiters (leaders in Gaue — similar in size to electoral districts)

760 Kreisleiters (leaders in Kreise — circles within the Gaue)

21,354 Ortsgruppefuhrer (leaders of local groups within the Kreise)

70,000 Cell Wardens (leaders of street cells)

400,000 Block Wardens (leaders of smallest unit — blocks of flats or houses

B. THE S.A. AND THE S.S.

1

1 The *S.A.* (Sturm Abteilung or Storm Troopers) were Hitler's private army. Its members were drawn from the working class and were socialist in their views.
2 The *S.S.* (Schutzstaffel or Protection Squad) were the better-educated elite who acted as Hitler's personal bodyguard and took an oath of loyalty to him alone.

C. ORGANIZATIONS LINKED TO THE PARTY

1 The German *Labour Front.*
2 Nazi *Organizations of teachers, doctors, lawyers, professors, engineers and civil servants.*
3 The *Hitler Youth Movement.*

The Party organization was later expanded to cover all Germans in occupied territories. Gau 43 was introduced to cover these.

Party organization

communist members were imprisoned. It passed a law allowing Hitler to rule for four years without consulting it. Only the Social Democrats voted against it. (D4) Hitler could now act. He outlawed all parties except the Nazi party. The Reichstag passed laws to cover his actions. Within a year the *Reichsleiters* (departmental heads of the Nazi party) dissolved the elected state assemblies, and local councils disappeared. Power had slipped into the hands of the Nazi Party.

The party organization Hitler had so carefully developed in earlier years had taken over and its network of officials covered the country. (See diagram above) The activities of every citizen could be reported to the Gauleiters who had full powers to carry out Hitler's orders.

Joseph Goebbels, Minister of Propaganda, said there was nothing to fear. The Party, he said, stood for love of Germany; freedom and bread for all Germans; and the common interest before self-interest.

After a triumphant celebration of National Labour Day on 1st May 1933, in which workers' organizations took part, Hitler gave orders for the offices of the trade unions to be attacked and their funds confiscated. He brought both the unions and the employers' organizations under his control. Politically and economically the country was now in his power.

THE NAZI PARTY AND THE NIGHT OF THE LONG KNIVES

The Nazi Party had enormous influence on the lives of the people. All professional people had to join Nazi organizations. Children were drafted into the Hitler Youth and taught to obey their Leader unquestioningly. Through the Labour Front, the Party demanded loyalty and dues from the workers. Only from within the Party was Hitler's position challenged, by the S.A. (see diagram on page 6) whose ready use of force had helped him to power. Its members were jealous of the influence of the S.S. (a new group) and impatient to carry out a 'second revolution' — that is, the establishment of the socialist state mentioned in the Party programme.

Hitler had no intention of introducing socialism, and he ordered the S.S. to assassinate the leading members of the S.A. These killings took place on 30th June 1934 and this date is known as the Night of the Long Knives. At the

Cartoon showing a wealthy Jew enticing an Aryan woman

same time the removal from industry of radical Nazis who wanted to take over the employers' associations seemed to end any idea that the Party would control the economy.

THE PARTY AND THE GOVERNMENT

How were the tasks of government and party separated in Nazi Germany? Hitler stated in 1935 that he expected the government to continue to administer the State organization while the Party educated the people in Nazi ideals and trained them in obedience. (D5) In certain areas control was clearly set out. The Party was all-powerful in education, culture and the Hitler Youth. It was also strongly linked with the Labour Front. The Government controlled the armed forces and the labour service. Recruits gave up their Party membership during their labour service. Elsewhere it was less clear who was in control and there was constant friction between the Party and the Civil Service.

Many Party members occupied high posts in the Civil Service and in other State bodies. Party members entering government service generally became less Party-minded and were often those who had joined the Party late. After the war started, however, an increasing number of S.S. members were employed in high posts and gained great power. State control over Party members was difficult since the Party had its own courts in which members had the right to be tried.

EIN VOLK, EIN REICH, EIN FUHRER *(ONE PEOPLE, ONE NATION, ONE LEADER)*

To make sure his power lasted, Hitler set out to win control over the hearts and minds of the people. He repeatedly told the Germans that they were special. He called them Aryans and pictured them as tall, handsome, blond and physically strong. He encouraged them to believe that blood and soil had made them the most cultured and kindly people who put the welfare of the community first and were morally fitted to lead the world. (D6)

Hitler said the British and Americans were acceptable people but the Slavs (Russians, Poles and Czechs, etc) were fit only to serve the Germans. He classed gypsies and Jews as sub-human. (D7) He taught that the world would benefit from Aryan rule. Hitler therefore believed his first duty was to unite all Germans, whether they lived in Austria, Poland or Czechoslovakia. Under his leader-ship they would form a community which could stand against the world.

The Nazi Party was responsible for seeing that children absorbed these ideas through the Youth Movement. At eighteen most of them were convinced Nazis. Boys then went into the S.S., the Army and the Labour Front for the rest of their lives. The community was to consist mainly of healthy, strong young people dedicated to National Socialism and Hitler. The aged, the mentally ill and the diseased were to be put painlessly to death.

Nazi leaders: on the right Dr Goebbels, Minister of Propaganda; in the centre Adolf Hitler ; on his right Hermann Goering, Hitler's deputy

HITLER'S CHIEF MEN

Most of the Nazi leaders did not look like ideal Aryans nor did they behave as the great cultured people they were supposed to be. Most of them could best be described as gangsters. They enjoyed and misused their power. Many became rich at the country's expense. Hermann Goering grew lazy and immensely fat and wore extravagant clothes (D8) and held hunting parties where the beaters dressed in medieval costume. Heinrich Himmler, Reichsfuhrer of the S.S., was described as 'half schoolmaster, half crank'. Mild and harmless looking, he was responsible for thousands of deaths in the concentration camps. Reinhardt Heydrich was a fine violinist. He carried out his orders to destroy the S.A. without any apparent feeling. Out of a long list Goebbels was the best educated. But bitter about being a cripple, he managed the propaganda, twisting the truth without conscience when it served his purpose.

HOW DID HITLER KEEP CONTROL OF GERMANY?

Hitler and his men ruled by keeping most of the people occupied with work, party activities, meetings and parades. Many were happy to be playing a part in Germany's revival. The voices of their leaders urged them on from loudspeakers and radio sets, and no criticism of the government appeared in the press. The architect Albert Speer, stage-managed superb parades and torch-light meetings, full of colour and martial music. At open-air meetings thousands of swastika banners, standards and uniformed men stretched into the distance, demonstrating the new power of Germany. By 1936 most Germans felt secure. Lloyd George, British Prime Minister during the first World War, visited Germany in 1936 and wrote enthusiastically about what he saw. (D9)

For those who opposed the system or got in the way, there were other methods of control. The Gestapo (secret police) kept track of them. The S.S. (black-shirts), specially trained to be tough and obedient, (D10) terrified them. These smart-uniformed young men swaggered along the streets, singing violent songs, often directed against the Jews. If ordered to do so, they would beat,

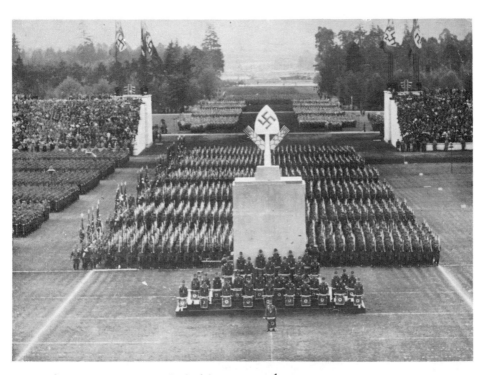

Part of a great Nazi parade held in Nuremberg

Jews behind the wire of a concentration camp

torture and kill. The People's Court, under its dreaded judge, Freisler, offered no protection. Beyond it lay the concentration camp with its slow starvation, medical experiments, gas chambers and mass graves. (D11) Into the camps came Communists, trade unionists, resistance workers and — in their thousands — the Jews. Most of them never left alive.

WORKING IN THE REICH

Hitler put Hjalmar Schacht in charge of the nation's finances. He quickly supplied the 'work and bread' promised by the Leader. Unemployment was reduced from six million in 1933 to half a million in 1939. People found jobs in the Nazi Party, in public works programmes (including the

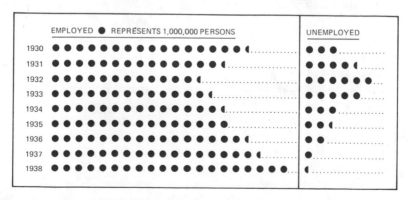

Employment and unemployment 1930-38

Volkswagen poster — 'You must save 5 marks a week if you want to ride in your own car'

building of autobahns — the first motorways) and in the growing armaments industry run by the Krupps family. Others joined the Gestapo, the S.S. and after 1935 the rapidly expanding armed forces.

By the middle 30s, however, there was a labour shortage. Workers in important industries such as metal and building had to get permission to change their jobs.

Wages were not high but the workers were in good spirits. Industry continued to expand and to recruit more women. To increase self-sufficiency, some products like rubber began to be produced artificially.

Increased output was encouraged by the 'Strength through Joy' campaign. Workers' contributions to the movement could gain them a home, a car, a cruise or a theatre ticket. (D12) This gave them something to look forward to in spite of heavy taxes and dues to the Labour Front. Small businesses suffered and about 10,000 were forced to close in Berlin alone. The owners were often drafted into the armaments industry.

In the countryside a great deal of work was carried out by young men doing their six months Labour Service. They lived in military-style camps. (D13) German farming had been relatively backward. The Reich Food Estate now encouraged food production by setting quotas and fixing prices. The Hereditary Farm Law attempted to prevent the land being divided into small units. It stated that a farm should be inherited by the eldest son, providing he was 'peasant-worthy'.

Libraries, clubs and entertainment were started to make country life more exciting. In spite of improvements, however, workers drifted from the land to better paid jobs in industry and the armed forces.

With the coming of war, the armed forces claimed many of the remaining male farmworkers, and the farms were often run by women with the help of prisoners-of-war or slave labourers from the east. The latter were underfed and were worked like animals on the land and in industry, with no thought given for their survival. (D14)

THE FAMILY

For the Nazis the main purpose of marriage was to produce a large, healthy family to provide the workers and soldiers Germany needed. People unlikely to have healthy children were often sterilized. Pressure was put on men and women to marry and raise a family. The single career woman and the childless wife were regarded as second-rate.

The birth-rate was encouraged by marriage loans to newly-weds, child subsidies to poor families with four or more children under sixteen, and family allowances. From 1939 onwards the Honour Cross for the German mother was presented yearly to women with especially large families. (D15) They became highly respected and had special privileges. The Nazi

The Iron Cross awarded for bravery in the German army

The Honor Cross of the German Mother, modelled after the Iron Cross

The Iron Cross and the Mother's Cross

ideal of the German woman was the simple home-lover, fond of neither fashion nor make-up, nor reading. Women were, however, pressed into the Labour Service, particularly during the war. Their health often suffered and the birth-rate fell. Relations between parents and children whose ideas were formed in the Youth Movement, were particularly strained in homes where parents were religious. The family had become too much a part of the State and lacked the privacy it needed.

THE YOUTH MOVEMENT

Hitler intended the young generation to become convinced Nazis completely loyal to him. Most of their out-of-school activities were organized by the Youth Movement. Outdoor exercise and camping fostered their health and helped to develop a community spirit. They learned the Nazi doctrine thoroughly, wore uniforms and swore to follow Hitler. Even the Pimpfen (boys of 10—14) took part in

Hitler addressing a meeting of the Hitler Youth movement. Behind him stands Rudolf Hess and, to his left, Baldur von Schirach

these activities and the length of their marches horrified some mothers. (D16) Boys and girls of 14—18 in the Hitler Youth competed in sport, music and even collections for Winter Relief. This occupied most of their time and energy, and they grew up restless but uncritical. At eighteen many of them were fanatics. Like the army and the S.S. they took part enthusiastically in great parades. Led by Baldur von Schirach, a soft young man who did not look tough enough, they saluted their Fuhrer, and sang their anti-Christian songs. They felt grown-up and important. (D17) Many parents worried as juvenile delinquency grew, but it was a young people's world and most of them found it exciting.

NAZI EDUCATION

The German schools also aimed at making good Nazis. All pupils, in day and boarding schools had lectures on the superiority of the Aryan race and of National Socialist principles. The material used for ordinary lessons such as mathematics and history emphasized these ideas. (D18) Boys' education leaned towards militarism, girls' towards domestic science and training for mother-hood. Lessons ended at 1.00 p.m. but sport and Party activities filled the rest of their day. Intellectual activity was despised. Educational standards declined even in the special schools for officials of the State and the army, as well as in the universities. Entry qualifications were health, racial purity and loyalty to Nazi ideas. Only

books approved by the Party could be studied. It was more important for teachers to belong to the Nazi Teachers' Association than for them to be good teachers. These policies led to a general lowering of academic standards and achievement. The Hitler Youth Law exempted able pupils from Party activities to allow them to study harder, but standards declined even further.

CULTURE AND ENTERTAINMENT

All permitted forms of art and entertainment were made to serve the Reich. Many of them were dull and unimaginative. In 1933 books containing ideas with which the Nazis disagreed were burned in public. This set the pattern. Press and radio were censored; theatres showed only safe classical plays; films reinforced propaganda. Music played in public was either martial or sentimental. The art galleries reflected Hitler's taste in pictures. None of the creative work approved by the State was of outstanding value, but many artists and writers worked in secret, waiting for the return of freedom.

RELIGION

The Nazi ideas were like a new religion. (D19) The Nazis thought that old religions, like Christianity, were out-of-date and a nuisance because they stopped men developing their full powers. Naturally there was trouble between the Nazis and the Church. In 1933 Cardinal Faulhaber of the Roman Catholic Church opposed

A pagan procession draws the crowds

Hitler's racial ideas; Christianity, he said, stood above race and taught that all men were equals. He urged respect for the Jews from whose religion Christianity had sprung.

There were churchmen, however, who were enthusiastic about the new Reich. Protestants, who wanted one church for the whole of Germany, started the National Church Movement in Thuringia. Some churches held services and blessings for the Hitler Youth in spite of their anti-Christian ideas. Young children at Nazi lunches thanked the Fuhrer instead of God for their daily bread. Though these things were disturbing, some Christians though Hitler was better for Christianity than the communists, and praised him for

Property defaced by an anti-Jewish slogan

defending European culture.

Churchmen who spoke against the State or the Youth Movement were sent to concentration camps. By 1941 Hitler was convinced that the problem would settle itself peacefully. The growing generation, he said, would ignore the Church, and congregations would be increasingly composed of the elderly. In the end the Church would die. Meantime paganism was growing. Girls in pagan costumes attended harvest festival ceremonies, and pagan inscriptions decorated the Hitler Youth Memorial Hall.

THE JEWS

In 1933 there were half a million Jews in Germany. Most of them were hard-working and successful. Many were rich. The country benefitted from their energy and ideas, but anti-Jewish propaganda made many Germans regard them as evil and sub-human. They were blamed for the loss of the First World War and the troubles of the 1920s. They were attacked both as communists and as capitalists. People were told not to buy from their shops. They were turned out of all official jobs and not allowed to join in cultural activities.

In 1935 the Nuremburg Laws took away their rights as citizens and forbade them to marry non-Jews. (D20) The wiser ones fled. Their property fell into government hands. Yet even after 'Crystal Night' in 1938 when their shops were stoned and synagogues destroyed, many still hoped for better days. Instead more and more Jews were sent to concentration camps. As German power spread, Jews in other countries also suffered. In Poland the Jewish area (ghetto) became their prison and often their grave. From 1941 all Jews over six had to wear the yellow Star of David. In 1942 leading Nazis worked out the 'Final Solution' — the death of

The 6-pointed yellow star
had to be worn by all Jews
over six years old from 1941

The 5-pointed red star
was the badge of the Bolsheviks
(Russian Communists)

In anti-Jewish posters and cartoons the Jew was often shown wearing the red star on his cap. This encouraged people to think Jews were all communists and enemies of Germany

all European Jews. The gas ovens of the extermination camps were designed to carry out the sentence, and six million perished.

WAR AND ITS CONSEQUENCES

In 1938 and 1939 Hitler's policy of uniting all Germans led to union with Austria and the invasion of Czechoslovakia and Poland. The Greater German Reich had become a reality. Hitler's New Order was imposed first on Poland. It was designed to reduce the occupied countries, especially in eastern Europe, to a position where all their resources and man-power would be used for the benefit of their German masters. (D21)

The invasion of Poland, however, brought war with Britain and France. Germany's aim of self-sufficiency, her need for war materials and her desire for extra

Czechs show anger and distress as German troops enter their country

The Reich at its greatest extent in 1942

living space led to the invasion of Russia. *(The Two World Wars)* Hitler hoped to gain the wheatlands of the Ukraine and the Caucasian oil wells. In December 1941 he declared war on the United States, trusting Japan to keep her busy in the Pacific. His ambition was never satisfied and led to a disastrous over-stretching of Germany's resources and manpower in a way she could not hope to win.

German factories, transport and cities were heavily bombed. Production was badly affected. With defeat in Russia, and the American and British landings in France in June 1944, total defeat grew nearer. Hitler gave orders to destroy all equipment and machinery. Some officers refused to obey these orders and the rapid advance of the Allies saved the last useless squandering of Germany's resources. (D22)

HITLER'S REICH IN WORLD HISTORY

Why should we study something as evil as Hitler's Germany? Firstly, the Nazis changed so much and killed so many people, especially Jews, during the war that we naturally ask why this happened. Secondly, we should understand that it was partly because of Hitler's ambitions that the present world came into being. The Second World War was fought to defeat him. Germany's defeat and division made the USSR the greatest power in Europe, and western Europe turned to the

19

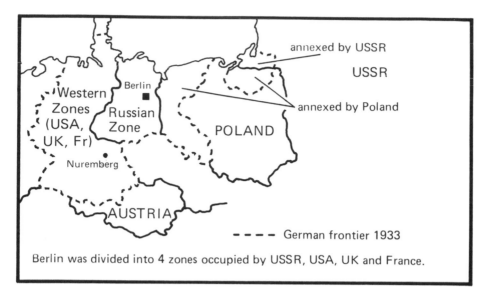

Berlin was divided into 4 zones occupied by USSR, USA, UK and France.

Germany divided and occupied in 1945

United States for help, thus setting the stage for the Cold War. *(The Cold War)*

Thirdly, the failure of Hitler's plans changed the map of Europe. Germany was partitioned and lost land to Poland. German colonies in eastern Europe were wiped out. Poles, Czechs and other peoples had had enough of Germans and turned them out of their countries. Fourthly, a lesson may be learned from looking at the organization of Hitler's Reich. In another booklet in this series the growth of the power of the State is described. *(The Growth of the State)* In the twentieth century, the State has acquired a new control over the lives of the people, but who controls the State? In democratic countries it is supposed to be the people. In Germany, a group who thought themselves better and wiser than the ordinary people claimed that they should control the State.

They persuaded a large number of people that they were right. In this way the Nazi Party gained control and used their power to impose on the people what the Nazis thought they ought to want. The awful results show the importance of working out how the great power of the modern State ought to be used.

Hitler's Reich had much in common with other countries between the wars. Like Russia, Italy and Spain, it had trampled on Parliament and was ruled by a dictator. Where it differed was in the belief in racial superiority which had such tragic consequences for the Jews and east Europeans. In every occupied country however, there were those who admired and worked for Hitler as well as those who gave their lives to destroy him.

The ease with which Hitler persuaded the Germans to part with their freedom is alarming.

Women who had collaborated with the Germans during the occupation being punished by their own people afterwards

When you read of the dreadful things the Nazis did, you must wonder why the people allowed them to go on ruling. One reason was their strength, since they controlled the police and kept watch on the army. Another is that most Germans were law-abiding and did not want revolution. A third reason is that many Germans thought the Nazis had done well in getting the country out of the mess it was in in 1932. Now the Germans had jobs, and business-men were making profits. Ordinary people minded their own affairs and did not see that much was wrong. Most of them did not want to read forbidden books and did not mind when told they couldn't. They knew something about concentration camps but not how bad they were.

Only after 1942 when the war had begun to go badly did the Germans wake up to the way things were. By then it was too late to do much about it.

DOCUMENT 1

HITLER'S APPEARANCE   *A German describing Hitler in 1939*

Hitler is not physically attractive. Everyone knows that today. But at
that time stories were circulated in the party and among sympathisers
about his deep blue eyes. They are neither deep nor blue. His look is
staring or dead, and lacks the brilliance and sparkle of genuine animation.
The timbre of his harsh uncommon voice is repellant to the North
German. The tone is full, but forced as though his nose were blocked.
Since then the voice, gutteral and threatening, has become familiar to
the whole world. It embodies the torment of these years. . . . Hitler's
physical appearance certainly does not heighten the impression made by
his personality. A receding forehead with the lank hair falling over it; a
short unimposing stature, with limbs somehow ill-fitting and awkward;
an expressionless mouth beneath the little brush of a moustache — such
are the traits of the outer man. His only charm lies perhaps in his hands,
which are strikingly well-shaped and expressive. What a difference to the
strikingly youthful, intelligent countenance shown in Napoleon's death-
mask!

DOCUMENT 2

HITLER THE SPEECHMAKER   *GREGOR STRASSER — A Nazi*

I have been asked many times what is the secret of Hitler's extraordinary
power as a speaker. I can only attribute it to his uncanny intuition, which
infallibly diagnoses the ills from which his audience is suffering. . . . [He
is] one of the greatest speakers of the century. . . . Adolf Hitler enters a
hall. He sniffs the air. For a minute he gropes, feels his way, senses the
atmosphere. Suddenly he bursts forth. His words go like an arrow to their
target, he touches each private wound on the raw, liberating the mass
unconscious, expressing its innermost aspirations, telling it what it most
wants to hear.

DOCUMENT 3

THE EFFECT OF HITLER ON THE GERMAN PEOPLE   *WILLIAM*
L. SHIRER — An American journalist in Germany in the 1930s

Nuremberg, September 4th.

Like a Roman emperor Hitler rode into this mediaeval town at sundown
to-day past solid phalanxes of wildly cheering Nazis who packed the
narrow streets. . . . Tens of thousands of Swastika flags blot out the
Gothic beauties of the place, the facades of the old houses, the gabled
roofs. The streets, hardly wider than alleys, are a sea of brown and black

uniforms. . . . About ten o'clock to-night I got caught in a mob of ten thousand hysterics who jammed the moat in front of Hitler's hotel, shouting: 'We want our Fuhrer!. I was a little shocked at the faces, especially those of the women, when Hitler finally appeared on the balcony for a moment. They reminded me of the crazed expression I once saw in the back country of Louisiana on the faces of some Holy Rollers [religious fanatics] who were about to hit the trail. They looked on him as if he were a Messiah, their faces transformed into something positively inhuman. If he had remained in sight for more than a few moments, I think many of the women would have swooned from excitement.

DOCUMENT 4

THE REICHSTAG HANDS OVER POWER   *JOSEPH GOEBBELS*

March 24th, 1933.

The Leader delivers an address to the German Reichstag. He is in good form. His speech is that of an expert statesman. Many in the House see him for the first time, and are much impressed by his demeanour. . . . The leader of the Socialists, Wels, actually returns a reply which is one long woeful tale of one who arrives too late. All we have accomplished the Social Democrats had wanted to do. Now they complain of terrorism and injustice. When Wels ends, the Leader mounts the platform and demolishes him. Never before has anyone been so thoroughly defeated. The Leader speaks freely and well. The House in is in an uproar of applause, laughter, and enthusiasm. An incredible success!

The Zentrum [Centre Party] and even the Party of the State [Staatspartei], affirm the law of authorization. It is valid for four years and guarantees freedom of action to the Government. It is accepted by a majority of four to five; only the Socialists vote against it. Now we are also constitutionally masters of the Reich.

DOCUMENT 5

PARTY AND STATE   *From an official Party report, 1935*

The task of the state is to continue, within the existing framework, legally to administer the state organization which has historically developed. . . .

[The Party's task is] first, to direct the efforts of its entire organization towards the establishment of a stable self-perpetuating and eternal cell for the National Socialist doctrine; second, to educate the whole people to this idea; and third, to hand over the people, thus educated, to the state for its leadership. . . . As to the rest, the principle of mutual respect must be observed by both jurisdictions.

DOCUMENT 6

ARYAN GREATNESS   *HITLER — From his book* Mein Kampf *(My Struggle), written in the 1920s*

The readiness to sacrifice one's personal work and, if necessary even one's life for others shows its most highly developed form in the Aryan race. The greatness of the Aryan is not based on his intellectual powers, but rather on his willingness to devote all his faculties to the service of the community.

DOCUMENT 7

ARYANS AND JEWS   *HITLER — In* Mein Kampf

If one were to divide mankind into three species: the culture-creators, the culture-bearers, and the culture-destroyers, only the Aryan would be likely to fit the first definition. It is to him that we must trace the foundations and the walls of all that human beings have created. . . . The most powerful antipode to the Aryan is the Jew. . . . No, the Jew possesses no culture-bearing ability whatever, since he does not, and never did, have that quality without which man cannot truly develop toward a higher order: idealism. Therefore his intellect will never act as a constructive force.

DOCUMENT 8

GOERING   *VON HASSALL — An anti-Nazi German diplomat and politician executed by Hitler in 1944*

Goering kept him [Minister Thomsen] a whole day, was very friendly, drove him about in the forest, and presented a grotesque figure. He appeared early in a Bavarian leather jacket with full white shirt sleeves. He changed his costume often during the day, and appeared at the dinner table in a blue or violet kimono with fur-trimmed bedroom slippers. Even in the morning he wore at his side a golden dagger which was also changed frequently. In his tie pin he wore a variety of precious stones, and around his fat body a wide girdle, set with many stones — not to mention the splendour and number of his rings.

DOCUMENT 9

A REVIVED AND PEACEFUL GERMANY   *DAVID LLOYD GEORGE — In a* Daily Express *article, 'I Talked to Hitler', 17th November 1936*

I have just returned from a visit to Germany. . . . I have now seen the famous German leader and also something of the great change he has effected. Whatever one may think of his methods — and they are certainly not those of a Parliamentary country — there can be no doubt that he has achieved a marvellous transformation in the spirit of the people, in their attitude towards each other, and in their social and economic outlook. . . . One man has accomplished this miracle. He is a born leader of men. A magnetic dynamic personality with a single-minded purpose, a resolute will, and a dauntless heart. He is . . . the national Leader. . . He is also securing them against that constant dread of starvation which is one of the most poignant memories of the last years of the war and the first years of the Peace. . . . The establishment of a German hegemony in Europe which was the aim and dream of the old prewar militarism, is not even on the horizon of Nazism.

DOCUMENT 10

TRAINING FOR THE S.S.   *An eye witness account*

Combat training is terrifying. Yesterday afternoon we watched horrific fights between specially trained Alsatian dogs and the Junkers. This took place in a large field sloping down to the lake. Four cages containing the dogs were brought out, and at a given signal the doors were flung open. The dogs threw themselves like mad things at the throats of our Tier-kampf candidates. The latter had absolutely no protection against the fury of the beasts. Their special training enables them to overpower the dogs after only ten minutes or so. But if they should make a mistake, the dogs certainly won't. One of the men has a torn shoulder, and blood spurted from the gaping artery. He insisted, however, that nobody harm the dog. I find this quite normal. These animals are worked up until they are half-mad; the consequences must therefore be accepted. This is the kind of exercise which contributes to the 'character-forming' process at Vogelsang.

Fresh instructions must have arrived from Berlin. The training is getting more and more tough, cruelly tough. Since September the number of accidental deaths has risen to thirty-two. As at Vogelsang, the Sonthofen cemetary is slowly filling up with little flower-strewn graves. The weak must go to the wall here. Only those who survive will have the right to form part of the National Socialist elite.

DOCUMENT 11

A TEENAGER'S INTRODUCTION TO CONCENTRATION CAMP
From a statement by eighteen-year-old Walter Kramer at American Military Headquarters in Marburg, Germany, September 1945

In Danzig we were unloaded onto old barges in which the water was twenty centimetres deep. One tugboat drew the four barges up the Vistula to the notorious concentration camp of Stutthof. The camp S.S. immediately took us into custody. They took everything from us; we didn't keep even a belt and had to fasten our pants with twine. They led us to Compound Three, designed for two hundred fifty men, but we filled it with nine hundred. There were only three-level bunk beds – four men on the bottom, three in the middle and three more on the top. I always slept at top, for at least up there you don't get whipped so easily by the compound superior. The first two days we got nothing at all to eat. . . . In a camp such as Stutthof where there were forty-five thousand prisoners nine hundred didn't matter very much. Everything to speed our deaths. . . . One evening we had just lain down in our bunks when we had to line up for roll call. We simply stormed out of the barracks and the billy clubs did their work. Then right about face and to the gallows; forty-five thousand men were kicked out of bed to watch a prisoner being hanged for violation of camp ordinance [rules].

DOCUMENT 12

'STRENGTH-THROUGH-JOY' CAMPAIGN – THE PEOPLE'S CAR
From a German newspaper, 2nd August 1938

As of August 1 (1938), the great savings programme for the People's Car 'Strength-Through-Joy' will begin. I herewith proclaim the conditions under which every working person can acquire an automobile.
1. Each German, without distinction of class, profession, or property can become the purchaser of a Volkswagen.
2. The minimum weekly payment, insurance included, will be 5 marks. Regular payment of this amount will guarantee, after a period which is yet to be determined, the acquisition of a Volkswagen. The precise period will be determined upon the beginning of production.
3. Application for the Volkswagen savings programme can be made at any office of the German Labour Front and of 'Strength-Through-Joy', where further details can also be obtained. Factories and shops can submit collective orders.
A Volkswagen for every German – let that be our aim. That is what we want to achieve. Will all of you help in that; it shall be our way of saying 'thank you' to the Fuhrer. . . .

DOCUMENT 13

THE LABOUR SERVICE   *An Australian view in 1938*

So far the service has been used mainly to reclaim lands that can be used
in the fight to make Germany self-sufficient in her foodstuffs. It is in
keeping with the Nazi cult of Blut und Erde (Blood and Soil) to bring
the adolescents into close contact with mother earth, and wrest waste-
lands away from destruction. There is something satisfying to them in
triumphing over Nature. There were marshes to drain, swamps and moor-
lands to clear, erosions to be stopped, canals and irrigation channels to
be built, land to be reclaimed from the sea, and public amenities to be
created. Eight million hectares can be won back to cultivation, cry the
leaders, four provinces the size of Saxony can be gained to the Reich
without any war save with Nature. . . . One of the most typical sights in
Germany is to come upon platoons of labour service men swinging along
country tracks with shovels carried like rifles at the slope, or to see
masses of browned boys working lustily in the fields and stripped to the
waist in all weather. In the remotest woods one sees a red flag with a
black spade worked in its midst and, as one approaches, a brown-clad
sentry smartly springs to attention and brings his aluminiumed spade to
the present, and somehow it does not seem absurd to be saluted with a
spade. . . .

DOCUMENT 14

THE GERMAN ATTITUDE TO THE SLAVS   *HIMMLER – In a
speech to the S.S. Troup Leaders, 4th October 1943*

What happens to the Russians, what happens to the Czechs, is a matter
of utter indifference to me. Such good blood of our own kind as there
may be among the nations we shall acquire for ourselves, if necessary by
taking away the children and bringing them up among us. Whether the
other peoples live in comfort or perish of hunger interests me only in so
far as we need them as slaves for our culture. . . . Whether or not 10,000
Russian women collapse from exhaustion while digging a tank ditch
interests me only in so far as the tank ditch is completed for Germany.
We shall never be rough or heartless where it is not necessary; that is clear.
We Germans, who are the only people in the world who have a decent
attitude to animals, will also adopt a decent attitude to these human
animals, but it is a crime against our own blood to worry about them
and to bring them ideals.

DOCUMENT 15

THE HONOUR CROSS OF THE GERMAN MOTHER *From a*
German newspaper, 25th December 1938

'The prolific German mother is to be accorded the same place of honour
in the German Volk community as the combat soldier since she risks her
body and her life for the people and the Fatherland as much as the
combat soldier does in the roar and thunder of battle.' With these words,
Reich Physician Leader Dr Wagner, head of the People's Health Section
in the Reich leadership of the party, at the behest of the Fuhrer,
announced the creation of a Medal of Honour for prolific German
mothers at the Party Day of Labour. Three million German mothers, on
the German Mother's Day in 1939, for the first time will be solemnly
awarded the new badge of honour by leaders of the party. . . The youth
above all must be brought up with a reverence for the mothers of the
people. . . . The young National Socialist will show his respect for her
through the obligatory salute of all members of the youth formation of
the party. . . . In addition, the wearers of the Honour Cross of the
German Mother will henceforth enjoy . . . such privileges as honorary
seats at party and government-sponsored gatherings . . . and preferred
seats assigned by conductors in rail coaches and trolley cars. Further
they are to be provided with old-age care and be given priority for
acceptance in homes for the aged. . . .

DOCUMENT 16

TRAINING FOR YOUNG BOYS IN THE YOUTH MOVEMENT
From a description by a German mother

A twelve-mile march [was] considered a mere nothing for boys who are
trained until they can make a march of fifty miles without other food
than the concentrated ration they carry in their packs. Nupp was
convalescing from a heavy cold but he was not excused the hike. He had
a severe relapse as a consequence. I told our doctor I feared the boy
would not be able to do the strenuous tasks required, and he gave me a
written statement to the effect that our son must be excused from the
more violent features of training. Later the doctor confided to me that
often after one of these lengthy marches he had as many as thirty boys
in hospital. . . . Pale-faced little fellows sometimes made a march of
thirty miles singing Nazi songs through the night, for their graduation
ceremony. The 'bloodflag', one of the gory banners saved from the
fighting days of the Party . . . always figures in these rituals. The boys
raise their hands and make this solemn oath: 'In the presence of this
bloodflag which represents our Fuhrer I swear to devote all my energies,
all my strength, to the saviour of our country, Adolf Hitler. I am willing

and ready to give up my life for him, so help me God. One People, One nation, One Fuhrer.'

DOCUMENT 17

ANTI-CHRISTIAN SONG *THE HITLER YOUTH – Singing at the 1934 Nuremberg Rally*

No evil priest can prevent us from thinking that we are the children of Hitler. We follow not Christ but Horst Wessel. Away with incense and holy water. The Church can go hang for all we care. The Swastika brings salvation on earth. I want to follow it step by step. Baldur von Schirach, take me along!

DOCUMENT 18

LESSON MATERIAL IN A NAZI SCHOOL *From a German autobiography*

I had no lectures that afternoon. When Klauss got back from school at five o'clock he bullied me into helping him with his homework. Glancing through his school books, I noticed again how different they are from those I had had only a few years ago. . . .

Here is a maths problem picked out at random: 'A Sturmampfflieger on take-off carries twelve dozen bombs, each weighing ten kilos. The aircraft makes for Warsaw, the centre of international Jewry. It bombs the town. On take-off with all bombs on board and a fuel tank containing 1,500 kilos of fuel, the aircraft weighed about eight tons. When it returns from the crusade, there are still 230 kilos of fuel left. What is the weight of the aircraft when empty?'

Here is another one I had to solve for Klauss: 'The iniquitous Treaty of Versailles, imposed by the French and the English, enabled international plutocracy to steal Germany's colonies. France herself acquired part of Togoland. If German Togoland, temporarily under the administration of the French imperialists, covers fifty-six million square kilometres, and contains a population of eight hundred thousand people, estimate the average living space per inhabitant.'

DOCUMENT 19

A NEW RELIGION *Plans for the destruction of Christianity and the establishment of a National Reich Church, from the 30-point programme drawn up during the war*

5. The National Church is determined to exterminate irrevocably . . . the strange and foreign Christian faiths imported into Germany in the ill-omened year 800.

7. The National Church has no scribes, pastors, chaplains or priests, but National Reich orators are to speak for them.
13. The National Church demands immediate cessation of the publishing and dissemination of the Bible in Germany.
18 The National Church will clear away from its altars all crucifixes, Bibles and pictures of saints.
19. On the altars there must be nothing but *Mein Kampf* (to the German nation and therefore to God the most sacred book) and to the left of the altar a sword.
30. On the day of its foundation, the Christian Cross must be removed from all churches, cathedrals and chapels . . . and it must be superseded by the only unconquerable symbol, the swastika.

DOCUMENT 20

RACE   *Extracts from the Nuremberg Laws on Citizenship and Race, 1935*

  1   The Reich Citizenship Law of September 15, 1935
ARTICLE II: (1) A citizen of the Reich may be only one who is of German or kindred blood, and who, through his behaviour shows that he is both desirous and personally fit to serve loyally the German people and the Reich.

  11   First Supplementary Decree of November 14, 1935
ARTICLE IV: (1) A Jew cannot be a citizen of the Reich. He cannot exercise the right to vote; he cannot occupy public office.
      (2) Jewish officials will be retired as of December 31, 1935. . . .

111   The Law for the Protection of German Blood and Honour, September 15, 1935
ARTICLE I: (1) Any marriages between Jews and citizens of German or kindred blood are herewith forbidden. Marriages entered into despite this law are invalid, even if they are arranged abroad as a means of circumventing this law.
      (2) Annulment proceedings for marriages may be initiated only by the Public Prosecutor.
ARTICLE II: Extramarital relations between Jews and citizens of German or kindred blood are herewith forbidden.
ARTICLE III: Jews are forbidden to employ as servants in their households female subjects of German or kindred blood who are under the age of forty-five years.
ARTICLE IV: (1) Jews are prohibited from displaying the Reich and national flag and from showing the national colours. . . .

DOCUMENT 21

HITLER'S NEW ORDER IN POLAND   *From documents used at the Nuremberg Trials of Nazi war criminals in 1945*

Poland can only be administered by utilizing the country through means of ruthless exploitation, deportation of all supplies, raw materials, machines, factory installations etc., which are important for the German war economy, availability of all workers for work within Germany, reduction of the entire Polish economy to absolute minimum necessary for bare existence of the population, closing of all educational institutions, especially technical schools and colleges in order to prevent the growth of the new Polish intelligentsia. Poland shall be treated as a colony. The Poles shall be the slaves of the Greater German Reich.

DOCUMENT 22

THE END OF THE THIRD REICH   *An American journalist writes of his impressions on returning to Germany in 1945*

I found little bitterness towards him [Hitler] when I returned to Germany that autumn (1945). The people were there, and the land — the first, dazed and bleeding and hungry, and when the winter came, shivering in their rags in the hovels which the bombings had made of their homes; the second, a vast wasteland of rubble. The German people had not been destroyed, as Hitler, who had tried to destroy so many other peoples and, in the end, when the war was lost, themselves, had wished. But the Third Reich had passed into history.

ACKNOWLEDGMENTS

Illustrations

List Verlag, Munich page 5; *Politische Plakate 1900-70,*
Anschlage page 12; *Quatre ans d'histoire de France,* Amouroux
page 21; Radio Times Hulton Picture Library pages 3, 9, 10,
14; Wiener Library pages 7, 11, 16 both pictures, 17, 18.

Documents

D3, *Berlin Diary,* William Shirer, Sphere Books Ltd; D4, *My
Part in Germany's Fight,* Goebbels, Hutchinson Publishing
Group Ltd; D10, 18, *Other Men's Graves,* P. Newmann,
George Weidenfeld & Nicolson Limited; D16, *No Retreat,*
Anna Rauschning.

Greenhaven World History Program

History Makers
Alexander
Constantine
Leonardo Da Vinci
Columbus
Luther, Erasmus and Loyola
Napoleon
Bolivar
Adam Smith, Malthus and Marx
Darwin
Bismarck
Henry Ford
Roosevelt
Stalin
Mao Tse-Tung
Gandhi
Nyerere and Nkrumah

Great Civilizations
The Ancient Near East
Ancient Greece
Pax Romana
The Middle Ages
Spices and Civilization
Chingis Khan and the Mongol Empire
Akbar and the Mughal Empire
Traditional China
Ancient America
Traditional Africa
Asoka and Indian Civilization
Muhammad and the Arab Empire
Ibn Sina and the Muslim World
Suleyman and the Ottoman Empire

Great Revolutions
The Neolithic Revolution
The Agricultural Revolution
The Scientific Revolution
The Industrial Revolution
The Communications Revolution
The American Revolution
The French Revolution
The Mexican Revolution
The Russian Revolution
The Chinese Revolution

Enduring Issues
Cities
Population
Health and Wealth
A World Economy
Law
Religion
Language
Education
The Family

Political and Social Movements
The Slave Trade
The Enlightenment
Imperialism
Nationalism
The British Raj and Indian Nationalism
The Growth of the State
The Suez Canal
The American Frontier
Japan's Modernization
Hitler's Reich
The Two World Wars
The Atom Bomb
The Cold War
The Wealth of Japan
Hollywood

DATE DUE